# Nuthouse Episode



Kinga Stefaniec

| ISBN: | Softcover | 978-1-5434-9070-1 |
| --- | --- | --- |
| | eBook | 978-1-5434-9069-5 |



Print information available on the last page.

Rev. date: 05/30/2018

**To order additional copies of this book, contact:**
Xlibris
800-056-3182
www.Xlibrispublishing.co.uk
Orders@Xlibrispublishing.co.uk
776447

This is collection of my poems written between 1998 – 2018. I wanted to tell my story with strong language. Poems tells about travels, fighting with loneliness, addictions and experience of mental hospital patient. In 2015, I was admitted to medium secure hospital in Bristol where I am still till present day.

I write all about struggling with isolation, recall trips, physical and mental trips. I write about drugs and alcohol openly as filters of reality. As a way of liberation from social norms and expansion of perception. Struggling with hangover and side effects, mood disorders and mental illness. Sleep deprivation, fasting and meditation to reach altered states of mind. States opened with chemical keys.

Crossing thin line of sanity, I enter world of psychotic correlations with identity, biology of sex and homosexual desire. I look at myself as a mixture of feminine and masculine. I explore the vision of mind and body itself as a part of a Universe. Micro cosmos of imprinted mind into whole. I am interested with gnostic conversations with God, existence of God inside myself, reincarnation and philosophy of Cosmic Energy.

I believe in role of language as a system of communication to represent the creation of my own reality, subjective vision of it. As a carrier of significant meanings correlated with words as separate realities containing whole Universe or simple existence.

The edge of sanity is also relationship with another woman. Toxic or unhealthy gay relationship, but presence of another human being itself is very important. Woman is a reason why I end up in asylum. It is always a woman, as a lover, as a mother or as a feminine part of myself. I often sexualise reality to give it a meaning as a human, as a woman. Life itself has got meaning and it is a wonder, miracle. Suicide, play with death to look into Death eyes, to play God with my own life. Life as a coded encryption of DNA with chemical keys to read it. Entering the Matrix, cracking the code.

Meaning of traveling, nomad lifestyle, being an adventurer and free spirit not connected with society, but still firmly living city life. Breathing the city as a creation, living organism, part of an identity. Culture versus Nature. Individual against the masses. Poet against the world and opposite poet connected with the Word.

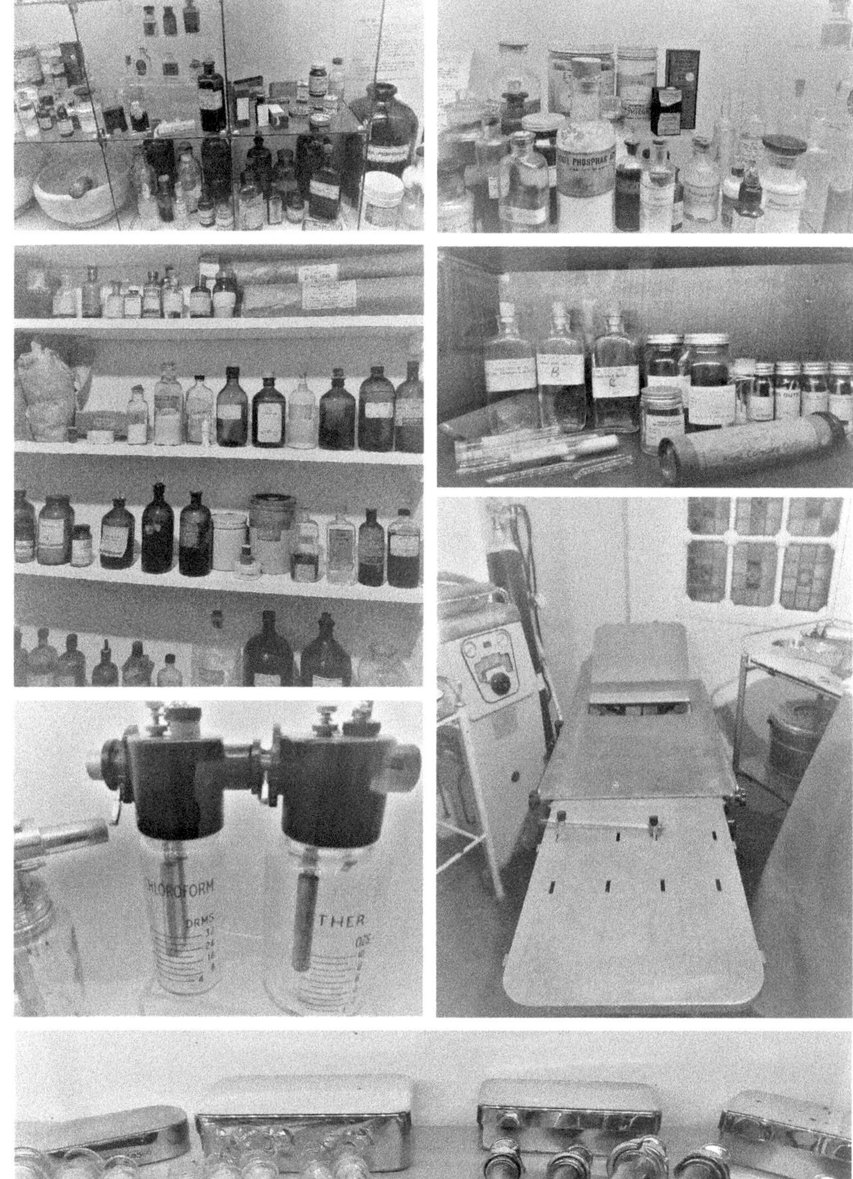
CHLOROFORM
DRMS

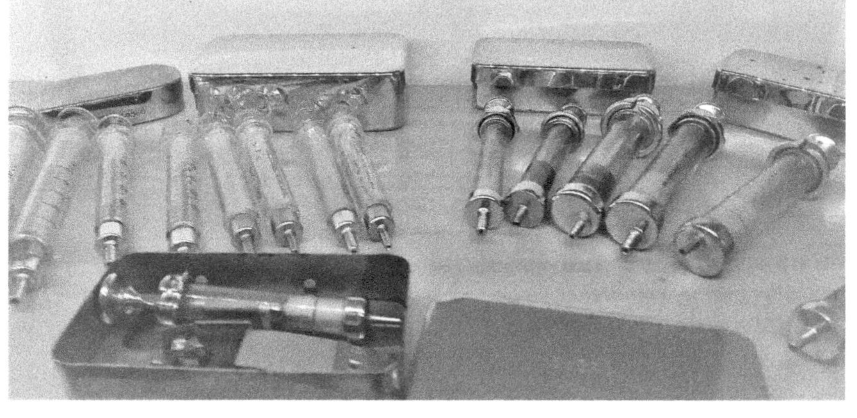

(Relanium words)

Black-and-white film in my head

It is like a sedative tablet

Dissolved under the tongue.

I've had enough pictures

I want to go

To the origin of the word:

I am. My course

Passionless route relationships?

Maddening confusion of

Movie lovers' perspective

Mirrors glued to the ceiling.

Caricature of paint spilled on a face

Again, it is only an image.

Of my thoughts.

[mypersonalobsessions]

Transcripts of experiencing the world

I want to expand

===== ====== internally for you

You use punctuation [stop]

[mypersonalobsessions]

== == stop

-

[pause]

== == stopplauz

9th dream irrelevant

I clench rim around each other

Ecstatic pressure hollows trails

Stray thoughts to a meadow.

Ninth dream last night

Suggests solution

Restless tremor,

I'm going against the tide,

I catch the bus to the depot

To walk back.

Go go go

Straight. Dictating the speed.

Street lights define something

Red… yellow…

No longer thought – go further –

Defy yourself on the other side.

Symbols matter.

I am going through streets whose names

They have been named

Only in my head

Go go go…

Asphalt move the shoes.

Beautiful night

Illuminated by the glow of electric

Lamp looks banal.

I clench rim around her.

Ecstatic pressure circulates in

Tired muscles.

This extraordinary lightness ankle

They carry themselves.

Go go go

Straight. Along the track electrical

Trams embedded in the story

This road without goal.

I clench ring around her.

Ecstatic pressure splatters

My thoughts accelerated.

Separation unconscious

After the sudden awakening of

Ninth sleep that night

It confronts the imagination.

I clench rim around each other

Ecstatically and consciously,

Because I like to put bad later.

Only fidelity naked soul

Saves in the electric city

Human embryo prior to an abortion.

I'm here.

I feel the smell of old bodies

Heated sodium lamp.

Artificial maintenance of cleanliness

Distracts from life.

I clench rim around each other

Ecstatic pressure

The only thing to personal behaviour.

Abnormality encirclement of the city,

Ravenous hunger for knowledge and change,

Questions pushing in hand

Additional written by others

Digestion thoughts.

I am doing my daily task

Tearing of the skin blood clots

Blood leaking from her nose.

She managed to carve connecting

The mouth small recess

Unfamiliar destination.

I clench rim around each other

Ecstatic pressure splatters

Droplets of mercury

The temperature crashed to the floor.

Minutes after the first

I breathe burned methane.

I clench ring around her.

I close the window

Not dream nothing.

***

Aldous Huxley:

*'(...) the urge to escape, the longing to transcend*

*themselves if only for a few moments,*

*is and has always been one of the principal appetites of the soul.'*

Bits of cosmos

Chunks of universe

I swim in a stew

I bite my nails sucking blood to the bone

Forgotten writing, sculptures made of words

Nest build of hungry thoughts

That's reality absinthe

Equal of nothing - green hallucination

Close encounters with awkward loneliness

Locked up in mental institution

Lunatic is on the grass!

Imprisonment in first impression

Love from the first sight

Trapped in bizarre love triangle

City divided on particles

There is no way out of the game

Policeman knocks to my door

Wires in my body silver antenna

Connects me with Idea

Police state doctors' opinion

I am going AWOL

Reset of system… repeat

Reset of system

Power blackout pause in my curriculum vitae

Mission failed, but who is on the other side of the phone?

Bearpit Story

This is Bearpit story

In old double-decker, I spent cold, winter night

Breathing air of 1960s to my lungs

Punk Paul converted bus for a squat

Hipsters converted squat for a coffeeshop

In a subway Zack plays guitar

Francine is clearly drunk she sits on a floor

Throwing food around

Behind her back Relentless Optimism -

Graffiti on a wall

Mandy is dancing with her bottle of wine

Punk Paul told me today I look like potato

And that he needs a shower

He will stay forever here

I teach them how to smoke pot from Polish pipe

It is not easy they swallow ‘devils’ instead of smoke

(Devil is red hot ash) I laugh

I shoot a picture tonight

Of all murals and posters

I shot line of ketamine

And I am fucked up

This place is a heart of the city

Arteries of subways with blood flow

Of people just passing through

From Broadmead to Stokes Croft and back

Sometimes someone gives me spare change

To exchange it for a booze in liquor shop

## Behind Glass

I live

Behind glass of oxygen mask

And outside air contaminated

Breath of tramps who twisted scar mouth

Set from the window wrapped in cloth with rain

Yes! Take a rain as well!

Natural expression of mourning clouds kicked in the stomach

I live

Behind a glass of screen that looks like a street

And the blinds passing crowd towards the church

All the tears to reach the door

And to know the truth

(from within speaks unnamed chuckle)

I draw signs with my finger on the glass

From the window of my room is still the same view

You would die of boredom

Bridge 9

Everything I experience turns out to be an illusion. Scars are true.

They recall that the past happened.

Soul on the shoulder I have. I'm all build from the wounds. And bitter

Taste on the tongue. You ran once the sea? I feel like

Clown on the ruined bridge. I dance amid mist of the shooting stars…

I shoot into the sky. I catch the eye sinking light flashes. Lose eyesight.

Will you be my guide dog?

I'm in brackets… I lose myself in quotation shred…

Collective unconscious... I lock myself in quotes like

Old movies in black and white. Colour moves on the form.

Structure of the face Marlene Dietrich in a cloud of smoke. Blinding contrast.

Spotlight and face of Marlene breaking the darkness.

Close to the structure. Not all… I'm not interested in a whole.

To me it is located on the border of black and white. On the border

Of blinding white face linking with the darkness. This point.

Your face has a similar structure. Please draw me all the sadness

In your eyes. Select all inequality of character. I hide everything in my pocket

And I pull out when you cry. I will rotate in the memory each moment

For whenever I want.

'Mom, do not feed me more, because I vomit.' All my mothers

In which the body is hid overfeeded me with hysteria. And me

Enough time heat get under the covers and feel the pulsating heat.

I shut of the heating. I'm still freezing regardless ambient temperature.

Wading ankle-deep in a swamp. Sensing life in depth.

Hesitation and simply lose lose even one step. I'm wading foot.

I'm all charred paper. Burning book. Unable to defend.

Opening periods interspersed with autism. Bogged down further.

Waist. The neck. Last breath. Water flooding my mouth.

I open the gills. Breathe water. Mired even deeper.

I clench your hands-on drifting the remains of life. Sky closes.

I go down to the inside.

I run away as Orpheus. I'm looking in depth. And I know the ending.

Let my heart break.

## City Lights

Big city lights

I take bath in a light

Of the city

I feed my cravings

Sleeping on a pavement

My body and body of a city

Is one body

Street flows in my veins

I eat graffiti for breakfast

Human traffic is my supper

Cars clogs my arteries

Tower blocks chain connects my head

With open sky

I live in a big city

Homeless

Crazy

Nuts

## Dissolved Sun

I look –

Lying on a back

Following the movement of air

In the branches of drawing clouds

forces the pressure

watery lines connecting

my woody body

running underground channels

pours sand between toes

the hourglass

I write in memory of each grain

Transparency distorted

Noise rebellion scream

Laughter silence

I am bending over backwards

I dip hands in the fire

Sparks

I immerse yourself in the heat of the whole

Breaking the beam –

I dispersed unnecessarily

Magic paint marks on the body and face

Breathing a mixture of rain

And grass clippings

Extends softly donut flower

Orange glow background unbuttoned over the city

Sweet cotton raspberry juice

Drip thick drops in the mouth

Swallow gaze atmospheric discharges

I paint the sky magical characters

Sun cut in half

I put under the tongue dissolves with effervescence

## Dream Machine

My mind is empty
In an emptiness swim
Brain of the Universe.

My mind is in blackness
Shooting with stars
As an electric rain
to connect weeping surfaces of the rivers
with the skies.

Blackness of night surrounds me
I'm emptiness
There is no wind here
There is no light
I'm heavy and in deep sleep
Dreaming the Eternity.

## Ecstasy asylum

Whole hour sitting in lotus position

Waiting in my body mist for

Ecstatic rush makes my thoughts race

I'm crushing in the same car

I'm crushing in the same car

Two years in the cuckoo's nest

Back in the garden where full moon

I vape orange fluid

I vape my period blood

I'm bleeding periodically

To remind my feminine part of my brain

About unborn baby living in my uterus

Tonight I'm high on a pill

I clench my teeth feel bitterness in my throat

Mental asylum on pills

In green straight jacket in padded room

I'm crushing in the same car

I'm crushing in the same car

Door without handles

Yellow papers

Restricted items

Injections

***

On duty at night

Wrapping nightmares with a blanket

Tame dragons

Rhymes fairy tale

Fill space

They wake up fairy

Dusty imagination

Hocus pocus boom!

Regained magic power

I cast the spell yourself

Destroying castles in the air

Safe Mode releases energy

Changes dampens anger

Gently go into state

Neutralize the lulling pain

The strings wind float

Sending letters in the sky

With childlike rhymes

- Ene-due-rabe…

Here words have the power to create

Worlds of their own providing

The levels of learning to fly

Enchanted bottled illusion

Lens in the world refraction sunlight

Masked grey flicker

Colour stacking capabilities

Shades reflected in the iris

what is the conclusion?

It fell from the sky like cloud

Covering my eyes

Esprit de corps!

I feel the continuing lack

Permanent lack of sleep

Hunger and cold

And the worst is lack of the rhythm

Audible inside the body

There is artificially stimulated

TV

Purely and without control

My body is a weapon against himself

By passionate heartbeats

They filled every minute on average 75 times

Until the heat wave from the stomach through burned

Lungs came through the throat and floods all around

My esprit de corps!

Convulsions in the morning wipe the brutal conversation

Passing day

Clear fingerprints on the glass

Like a strange state when flowing out of the water

Without metaphors caught me thought that bounce off the surface

And dive deeper to find the start of air bubbles

This is not true lie

I drink vodka my esprit de corps and a sense of themselves

If I have to define it?

I ask for a long time

Drinking to myself to call

Sad clown related convulsions body of the town Zabrze's

Sweep of the soul more and more drunk hearing pushed back

The wall itself without suspicion and subtitles

Striking head like an alcohol

Worse is when I walk down the street and everywhere attack dead drunk

Creeping out of the gate

Street all the rocks in the wild rhythm of burned body

Lying on the sidewalk

The breaks fall asleep and the brain registers

Esprit de corps!

Impromptu soul is racing with vodka infused esprit de corps

Detention in the mouth accelerates the outflow inside

So I keep breathless until the liquid sultry cuts protein

Language and crumbles delicacy cheeks

How they hurt my ears from the superheated air

And hand touching the forehead waiting to explode lived

Blue clear sins of piercing the skin

Whole out of my mind and I look forward to sleep

Which lingers staring in absolute

Emptiness and bizarre music inside

As naturally is subjected to primary reflexes

Its body when envelops the mind

Amazing retreat to embryo where only the rhythm

And darkness dictated reflex digging

## Explosives Under Special Supervision

Glassy jade green radiance had exploded into field of vision

My head related to bunch of electric dreadlocks

Inserted to the Head of God Dog

Metallic drains high – voltage lines shining with colour of glassy jade flashes data's.

I was not there

I was enslaved with bunch of minutes shortened by blood flow of letters

Lightning greens of trees turn into golden – reddish leaves

- Perpetuum autumn –

River silvering as mirrors catch up last sunrays in fish bodies

Lay on a side all shines with light…. Silver and red spots of colours named to

allow me think more about

Faults sinking into blueish waters flushing emotions out of mind

Own language construct structures of communications between living things

Blasting bombs carrying heavy sins mourning with full moon

Last drops of sleeping sun on a top of a trees

Grass turning purple – orange plots under pressure of coming night

Freezing winter inside flesh

Blood cells stopped to feed this iron weapon to cut of heads

Crucify thoughts

In proportions and measurements now unimportant.

Kingships dies on red carpets stabbed with blade

See spectrum of reality in square tiles 3D

Alternative realities stretched on a screen

All hidden in a dust of explosions cheerfully and brightening

Everything is everywhere

Feel conscience of universe in that single moment of divine madness

To be divided in schizophrenic act of mindless crime

Descending greens of trees points old decades turning into precise electronic clusters. Connected to brain of universe. Read: head of squatters – base of files ready to be checked –

Refurbish from rubbish

Surfing into space – sending impulses from head to toe

Makes it alive and thinking even more…

Reach out weak explosives to detonate

Infrared Eye on forehead of enlighten Man to survive destruction of religions

Made by God Dog whose finger made red hole on a forehead to squeeze out juice.

There is no end of it.

## fingerprints

I got a book 'Seven Years in Tibet' from the flea market

Carry in my backpack from town to town

I'm a wanderer never sleep twice in the same bed

Homeless on streets of Paris London & Amsterdam

Hitchhiking at night to get to the point

To cover anxiety of being

I follow my own footprints in the snow

Trajectories of roads

& railways

To travel without a ticket

Imprinting vision with landscapes of cities

Tower blocks bridges canals

Saving sense of smell of city's garbage and rain

I collect city fingerprints in my laptop

Like evidence of crime

Police interrogates me under street lamp

Night in custody

Handcuffs like wedding rings

Of my slavery

Blue neon red door grey walls

Talks with advocate through the intercom

Howling inmates tattooed policeman

I am in hellish absence of mind

Man in black suit takes me on a ride

Police follow that van

## Full metal straight jacket

System wants to break me

Pulling the alarm

Nurse is checking me every 15 minutes

Looking into my eyes with cold torch

Drug screen if I'm clean

I need a cigarette

I need all poisons to intoxicate my body

To have a fit

To have a blackout

To start fresh to reset the system

In years of soberness I had no illumination

I want to see God's face in peyote jelly button

Whole life has its holy contour

Holy patients in holy asylums

Holy prisoners in holy jails

I get injection to calm down my psychosis

In full metal straightjacket I wait

chewing bubblegum like a soldier

at night wait for a sunrise

to kill the enemy in me

## God Bless Avenue

Surrounded by force shields
Wrapping our fragile bodies
We scratch imagination walls like animals
Making scarifications on a skin of Reality.

Alternatives lead to the point
Where we meet past lives.
According to another dimensions
Visible in healing crystals left on a table
Mirrored Lights produce rainbow dreams
Ready to cook brains.
Table is black like a night sky
Scratched as shooting stars marks my way
To the room in the attic with yellow walls
Large window is like a flat TV screen
We sit on Ikea couch smoking hash from glass pipe
Letting the ash fall to the vintage red and white
Marlboro ashtray stolen from my parents' house
Watching the street's night life
Tramp collecting aluminum cans
Neighbour walks his dog
Drunk gypsies coming back from the bar singing loud
Since I saw your face my travel became a race.

## Henrietta Chinaski

I slept long

Woken up with hungover

late afternoon

She prepared eggs

I pour wine to the glass

Let's dance again

Dummy stuffed with raspberry cotton

In front of my eyes drunken dance

She takes off her skirt showing me legs

'Do you like my legs?' she asks

In double surface of the bottle I can see

Her face reflecting on both sides of the mouthpiece

I play saxophone on my bottle

I play a fool of myself

Drunk as fuck

Let's dance

The saddest song of this Christmas

## Hitchhiker

I wake up early with the sun

Wait on a motorway with thumb up

I'm the reincarnation of wanderers

Beatnik is in my soul

I slept many nights dreaming about a road

Travel is in my blood

To move forward is an urge

I can't resist

To wake up early with the sun

Wait on a motorway with thumb up

Cheap hotel room is my home for one night

All I possess is in my backpack

I have noting and I'm happy

Happy to hit the road

## Hour of Thoughts

Hour I

Clockwork blood flow velocity

Sleepless trance

Hour I

Substance nourished own sweat

Connected to a live body fluid

Hour I

Excavated from the tomb

Death's – head gas

For a minute I

Breath flooded lungs

Sometimes I am

Severed head

The rest is silence…

When the fifth time I am born out of a chair

Mind is a space -

Swims in a stew of virtual reality

Linked to the God's computer

He is a Holy Hacker of consciousness

Reaching out other Galaxies -

networks of multiplied solar systems

like spider webs

Modem in a brain

Dial connection with Universe

To jack in into net browser

Mind is a space -

Micro cosmos of God's dream

Holographic picture

Where what we see is a scheme

Matrix of flashing data

Mathematical wonder of letter fi

& serpent of DNA –

The key

## mind vs universe

In the rhythm

My body dances

To the melody of the rain

I squeeze duvet between my fingers

To soothe myself

Mindfulness practice

Meditation

Mediation between my mind and universe

Black holes of my eyes

Drowning world

In my eyes disappear

Through retinas

door

To the other side

To see

I open my eyes

To catch sunrays

Blind light in the mirrors

You can see my soul

Clear and pure

Heavy

I manipulate the light

Trapped inside me

My head is Sun

## My room centre of Earth

My room is my cell

With window in a door

For nurses to look inside

I barely wake up off my bed

Spending most time here

Familiar angles tv books

Sometimes at night I can hear

Engines smell of petrol

Tall fence isolate me from the world

Rest of the world is just peripheric

It is just illusion

My reality is hard as wooden stick

Of thought under the head

Like a pillow I hold it every night

Sleepless nights

I know all cracks on a ceiling of my room

I build construction of my books

To decorate raw environment

Fifteen steps from door to the window

Outside just tall fence

Fence is black and steel connected with alarm

To not go on a run when I like

To stroll on a meadows swamps

Hitchhike far from here

Nude body of reality

When I woke up this morning

I found her next to me

Laying like a prostitute

Nude body of reality

'Send me signal from a cloud factory'

- She said

'I love the Lord on high.'

In a wormhole

We ate our hearts alive.

That night in Amsterdam

I looked at the moon with new eyes.

offline

I am switched off

Unplugged from electricity

disconnected thread of spiderweb

Naked thread

I do exist in no time

Sculpting in mud body artwork

Printed words produce my own world

Language waterfall to name it as I want

Chopping wood in a cave to make a fire

Boil black coffee and take a rest

Watching game of dancing shadows

Audience sits back to the entrance

Like platonic cave theatre must go on

My street

Frontons of houses fake

Actors play the game watching the TV

My street is a theatre

I watch game of shadows through the window

It all doesn't make sense to me

Fake traffic fake cars fake scenography psychotic film

Who is the Director?

## Out of body experience

Telephone rings dryn dryn

Hellooooooooo

Her voice faded into nothing

I - suspended near ceiling

deliberately free

talking rubbish

talking trough laughter

my head is chopped off my body

I glance at myself

lost words faded into nothing

I was only an eye hanging under the ceiling

Out of darkness

My mind trapped in a game
Psychotic colours of machinery
Scratch the surface of Reality
I crawl like a baby on the other side
Of the canal breaking the membrane
bubble which I am in

In a stew crumbled brain
Microwaved

Don't hide the madness
In a nuthouse
- Doctor says
Injection in my ass
Tranquilize the plot
Head in orange bubble
Like space suit
Rapid tranquil kit tumble-dried
Soluble dream I swallow
It grows in my stomach
Relaxing muscles of my spine
I vomit moonlight river
I swim dissolved in a light

Completely

And I become a light

I become the psychotic colours

Of machinery

I scratch the face of reality

With my fingernails

## Parallel Distributed Alien Processing

In connections of thought produced by brain
Massive interactive network to simultaneously
Processes operate in parallel to result in it.
Connections of borders, action of migration
What is shared by nation by nation.
Me, locked in foreign land process foreign thoughts
Trying to connect with tamed island language.
In communication, peer to peer realisation
My alien self-started put down roots
Shy weak square roots attached city's underground
I am the origin of my young tribe.
Building shack in College Green
Squatting house in Portland Square
Inhabitant of Windmill Hill
This city one day will be mine.
All my life I have found small motherlands
My private lands who belong to me
Where I belong no matter what
Slavic soul connected with English language
On British land white eagle landed.

## Polish pike

Each day I travel to the point

That I don't know what to do with time

Each night I fall asleep late

When my soul travel to the other side

Now, I see silluettos faded in my dream

Head breaks the curtain of the edge of the world

Now, I know what is what

To travel is to leave the nest

Forget shower and warm bed

Sleep in a tent under black sky

Eat no meat

Boil black coffee in a fire

Burn lips with hot potato

I never clean dust off my shoes

Walking long distance on a motorway

And between is written down in notebook

Lonely journey through the fields of Europe

One day I will go further

To reach beyond my own limits

Princess On The Seed Of Grass

Balsamic shelter for my Slavic soul, wiping away everyday sins,

I'm blessed with a holy smoke –

Through open windows of my Slavic soul,

Vaporize sins to clear out luggage of possessed years.

Unforgotten yet. Heavy thoughts of mind closed in pendulum of sorrow

Injected to the veins poisoning whole system like polluted rivers.

Sad indeed, sad as my Slavic soul, so different here and quite sober

To contemplate landscapes of relationships, to resolve realities in parallel

Communicating with flesh. Stay in touch with conscious head.

My own hell – never classified with circles around my neck,

Tattooed deep rings as load of experience. Clearly,

They wanted me to be here

Without excuse, for being lazy in fact, for wasted public time. Sleeping deep.

At least life wasn't boring, now I must wake up, portfolio of dreams

Ready to show on a screen of my eyes. I'm spare part of the machine to produce

Good life for our masters, this makes me tired.

Tried to escape from the inside. Essentially nothing glued me here,

Except memories. Call it reset of system, death

New start, but I'm only spare part for a system, somehow

Always mostly looking for fun, travelling between destiny points. Current

Incarnation, as well, some connections made of scraps of

Experiences to fulfill meaning of peculiar chain of lives

I can feel it all, in my body, but

Somehow in sudden feeling, I'm sure that it all makes sense for now.

## Radiation

Green glowing light

Army of me

March of pigs

My head is hydrogen-bomb

World is spinning

Round and round

Tireless like electron

I can feel it in my feet

Radiation vibration

I feel I can collapse

My head is hydrogen-bomb

Ready to explode

I have to take painkiller

But it does not work

Target

War is not over

## ReaLithium

I can see layers of reality flaking of an ancient mural out of my eyes,

Mixtures of colours in prisms of falling raindrops.

When I can see you crying – the whole world is crying,

Washing out streets with rainbow rain all over again.

Flakes of fabrics forms new structures on a surface of your skin,

My dessert, where I climb to suck nipple,

To see my oasis in a sculpture of your body.

Rich, golden mind cells pays the price for being unlocked

From a heart of disease eating me from inside.

As bugs, rotten words bite layers of existence to uncover truths

So well – known for ancient poets.

To fulfill life with colours and songs as heaven's blues,

Melancholic patterns printed by hands of gods

To the forehead of modern slaves clinging with fake golden chains.

Unison played saxophones, shining in the sun,

Collections of items to fill up backgrounds

Of empty hours for everyman walking out through back door.

To remember faces of lovers evaporating through windows

In a light of torches carried by nurse to send message

Locked in crosswords made by system closure,

To find out what it means to be loved?

I've realized, no turning back to my dreams.

Monochrome movies in a back of my head,

To not forget silver faces on a screen, shining with pearls of tears,

Descended generations buried down in memory.

To create new town, absent of old habits

To not recall promises of failure.

Changing moods to proof surface of scenes ready

To show hidden scars healed under section in a nut house.

To feed zombies walking through my head, eating me brains,

Taking away sanity each time I allow to enter my space.

***

*'So far we have come. Here is solved*

*The end of the beginning.'* (Ewa Lipska)

Starry journey. Into chaos extracted from the throat of the soul. Dark

End of life. I move uncertainly in the new world of characters.

I collect the artefacts and the keys to my own consciousness. Scattered

Network events. I'm the beginning. Wanderer. Dusted shoes

Traces of hundreds of clues and acquired immunity. My personal identity

Bridge between the real and the internal. Self-eye perception

Senses. Memory. And the body shell of a network of neurons. Living

Hypothermic shock. The trailing step retrace

Each other. Diagnosis… eclectic string of associations with death.

Scored for hours' sunrises and sunsets. Catatonia

Sleepy duties. Internal clock breaks down in the face of

Aggressive image of the media. Rid of anxiety run

Further grasp of the situation by writing on the skin. Through the glass

Terrarium. I am the hundred characters and the key inside.

Scattered over meanings and the interpretation depends on the

Associations. Movement in space do not see

Personally. The reality is non-existent as time.

Transience addictive experience of rational strength of association.

I become yourself and discover meaning. Small marks on the

Hieroglyphs read out the skin and sucked blood will lead to

Strengthening using metaphors closure. The world inside

Extravert. Irony coated misleading laughter. Stream

I pour out on a paper stinging in the eyes. Slurred form

Spreads excess expressions.

Using metaphors movements. The only physical evidence

Life. I return to the beginning, to the inside where the embryo

Deliciously I stretched the time of birth. Memory left

Favourite reflex wrapping a pillowcase. And to the coiled

Carpet unnecessary body, amniotic fluid is gone. I'm leaving

Temporarily from the senses to fit in the distribution of time.

Distribution of flesh in a row. Between one stroke time

And the second followed by a string of events whose essence does not allow

Citation. Schizophrenic draft association puts me

In an illegal window space, recalling fragments

Conversations. Jerking hot sound waves. Eight-legged freak.

Off alarm. Mental shortcuts. Hairy wickets on the straight

Suddenly bend my horizon.

## Split Time Pieces

Sequences of seconds split time

Into pieces

I watch sand in hour-glass falling

My skin gets older

My hair turns grey

Traces of life grow on my face

I walk and the past walks with me

It lives

I need to prepare to die

Imagine my dead body in a coffin

Before I turn to life

I thought of time

## St. OK's Croft (enter the animation)

This town is a circle of madness
Spinning wheel with my body stretched on
Face bleeding after collision with political vision
Can't resist of fire burning inside chest
Have to score on St. Paul's and take a rest
Restore the generosity of spinning city
Unplugged from electricity
I'm knight on a bike too fast to push the brakes

My poems smell with black ink
Single letters grow as rain forests
Sit and watch life through blue cobalt glass
Touching words libraries networks
Deciphering Lumosity of ciphers letters
Smelling colours in it spotting brains with dirty water
Draining through shallow pipes forced to deliver point of view
To maintain circulating system of town
Hot springs in a shadow of fancy murals
Destroying whole city with fire and ash
Sick circumstances of Nature of things turn into mash
Dying connections with sense of being or humor set
To avoid turbulences during flight

Dead bored schemes messed by clusters of realicity build up with dump

Again stuck in mud of Turbo Island

Bypass masses of trained heads to cross borders

Already crushed with interior chaos howl from inside

Washed with drugs soul's insane tracks lost minds

Licking forehead of GodsDog in the hour of dead purposes unknown

Smooth glances of spotlight discover essence out of Ginsberg's poem

Melted in scream the same after decades of tortures\pin ups for travelers

Teachers blinded with perfection of world we live in

Now it's all doomed with shy farts pointed into unsure faces

Eyes wide opened for facts race is almost done

Fingers on belly button of this planet

Overeating resources to fire it

New is coming throw out religions keep it under carpet like dirty socks

Pervert visions of rocks rolling world as joint

Together pay bills for energy thrills

Wars unemployment social norms street art manners

Pointed to sting into public eye

In red hour of anger revolting thoughts to do it fast

Open wrists

Suck blood

Fried brains

Enjoy reddish dish tastes with colours of insanity

To feed hungry rioter in human multiplied by angry desires

Revenge of last generation on ancestors in grave

To show up grief of passed by days wasted by lack of loving letters

Sent by lover locked in mental asylum too busy to write back

All is soup of reality

Take me to the womb of my motherland

Where I belong no matter what…

## Suicide letter

No time is not the place. Illegally inside I produce myself.

Shots letting the other side. Word is deformed.

Erecting bridges letters. I am undressing letter into fragments.

Approximation. Chain letters. Following around the strings sequence

Time. Freely available manipulating reality –

I forgot to. Senses to become important is repealed.

The bending of the sine wave is touching her head leaning heavily ceiling

The walls. I deny everything spilling wine. Thickens

Blood with every sip. Thickens. Soon infiltrated density

Reinforcement of the building and bash about the words. Thoughts as red

Drops of wine. Blood. Paint. All characters have now made sense.

They are streaming down her face leaving a trace. Material of clothes is getting dirty.

They harden in the eye. Print I did on the retina. Glazy.

Kidding features albiotic bloodshot eyes. I follow the trail of

Blood mixed with wine on the most beautiful face that

Ever seen in your life. I stood among the lightning.

Over the trees doing the turnover among the leaves. Changing the distance

As needed. Freely. Casually turning angle

Tilt reality. She is asking childish questions

Glances of drops on her forehead too hard. I draw heat from the body

Next to weld together temporarily. Then I shut off treacherously

Weight. Eye – lost during drawing forgetting words.

Physical letters. Dimension. Style.

Collaborating with resentment kitsch colours available to me shapes

Unfilled contours. Filtration lung only material working.

Fuel muscles. Strongly taken out of context. Binding

Own mistakes in a silver frame laughter. Which is my right?

I conclude phrases random dot inspiration. Changing the syntax

I will replace meaning. Tomorrow will remain vague memory.

A sudden change of direction. Dot inhaling and exhaling commas.

If I sleep I live on the roof of the world. Narcissistically reviewing the

Polished scales of bullets aimed straight in the mouth.

I will be silent no longer. I spoke.

## Time squad

Spiritual ingredients cut with sharp existence blade

Fry gently in a flying saucepan imitating physics

Universal rules

'Stir well, serve on a hot plate of rushing thoughts.'

Caught in a meanwhile

Minutes falling from ceiling like drops of steam

Thick stormy clouds over our heads

Wet clay sculptures of junkies injecting heroin

Frozen in a pose

Of forever still (smack smelled with mud).

I was there

I have seen those atrocities with my own eyes

My heart is polluted with life

How to get out of the train?

## Trippin' souls

Climbing glass mountains

Explore empty rooms

Sandpits attics of my head

Recalling mems out of dreams

Projector lights pictures on a screen above

Flying soul's scent too strong to forget

Works as a button to recover files out of data base

Hidden in a head

Chain of coded meanings tattooed on a skin

With black ink to save the moments

Drunk souls trippin' in a light of holy night

Threesome foursome awesome

Glued together as atoms

Charged opposite in contemplation

Dialogues consistence

On top electrified atmosphere

Beneath hot

So slide down inside

Here

Now, in my body again

Pieces of puzzle game to reach Her

Future blank till very now

Could ask to watch Her while walk ahead

Focused on now and here

Suddenly I can see

Everything is everywhere

Is nothing

## Visions of Allen

Dear Allen Ginsberg,

You sit in a green automobile

Ride along wild river of Eternity

Buddha bells makes noises

And tambourine gently beat rain in my face

Allen Ginsberg,

You smoked marihuana leaves

To set up mind beyond

Allen Ginsberg,

You typed letters to your friend on benzo

To collect thoughts as sand on a desert

Allen Ginsberg,

You have long curly hair like a DNA serpent

You howl and scream in every line of your poem

You are buddha and yogini of words

You pray with smoke

You make love with sound of bell

Your green automobile dies in a horizon

You got six vaginas

in a process of homing the nervous system

Like a god of word, you spoke to me that holy night

To drink Eternity from the cloud of marihuana' smoke

Allen Ginsberg,

You ate spider web to show me affection

## Visions of french baquette

I sat high in a shore of Avignon's river

Scratching my toe to the bone

I sat drunk in a shadow of moon that night

Drinking rain drops falling to my mouth

I sucked leaves of the Tree of Life

Glowing green Oak –

And He spoke to me

Million voices among frozen bodies of stones

Faires living here

Shake electric feet

To talk to me with buzz of electric leaves

Of storm clouds

Where the river howl

I ate seeds of Datura plant

To see beyond the edge of Eternity

I read the Book to know

Me half naked looking through glass

Of a river's eyes

## Visions of Jack Kerouac

Jack Kerouac,

Why you put your words

Behind bars of Eternity?

Jack Kerouac,

Why no happiness taps from

Your lines of jazz?

Sleepless tensions of rhythm

And blues on your cards?

Metal typing machine blues

I can smell ink of your machine!

Jack Kerouac,

Why you are so sad in your vision?

Tender and gentle and sexy tribal singer,

Like Doctor Sax you print my eyelids with words.

Jack Kerouac,

You live a hermit existence in the darkness

Of his night.

Winter dream of Buddha Cat

Sober cold nights cover our hearts
Heads in clouds sprinkled with moon dust
Swimming around weightless bodies
No gravity to hold down to Earth

I'm in a tea room in Stokes Croft
'warm, spicy tea, please'
Milky drops baptize my head
I am a Dogsgod – the one who found few reasons
To incarnate again
To pick up healing herbs on my way home

Bare feet skip clear springs of hot blood
On a stoned path feeded with Lemon Haze buds
Warm winter I can't sleep again wind wakes me up
I'm surrounded by wiping walls
Long bright lighted halls of a nut house

I'm guest in my own dream
Sitting down in a waiting room
Help yourself with dried mushrooms

Play African drum-um-um till connection is made

Satellite sends joyful plans

All you must do is dance to love

The rhythm of your heart is a pure art

Rapid Tranquil Kit (inside a nut house)

I sit like a fetus inside shell of psychotherapy room
Recognizing voices coming out of my head
Conversations with myself help to spit out secrets

Cleaner polishes lino I can see my face
Reflected on a surface of the floor
Flashbacks of summer festival
I'm tripping again sitting in a shell
Like a young flower I grow on a meadows swamps
At least it is summer
This time of a year I hitch-hike
Somewhere to nowhere
With police vans ambulances emergency calls

Wrapped in walls
Electric locks tranquil pills
Pile of pills oily solutions injections to my ass
Occupational therapy saxophone lessons
Smell of saxophone on my hands smell of pills

Before I collapse to the lino floor I can hold world still
Fighting forces stronger than me

At least nothing happened yet

The world is standing still

Walking group dramatherapy bike project cbt

Vitamins antipsychotic pills black coffee pool

Rapid tranquil kid exercising freedom in dreams

black birds sit on black cordes of electric cables

black birds sit on a black cords of electric cables

around the city

smooth hands of wind play the song

black birds are black music notes system

this view is like a painting

I can see music as a river of black notes

played by smooth wind between hightowers of town

birds can sing violin notes in the time of sunsets

coloured by lights spreading horizontal bodies ahead

turning on brains like ear plugs full of music pictures

sliding in front of eyes as waterfalls intervalls

Imagine birds as notes on electricity bones falling to

The banks of river Avon shining rainbows

on a meadows interrupted by white blood cells of seagulls

ecosystem of Brizzle feed curious clouds on evening skies

dust falling on travellers heads

cargo boxes and lights of distant town

alive somewhere far

quiet needle to knitt fabric of landscapes

full scale of colours

smell navy blue greenish ocean

pick up words as notes

boxing with me

I've put you in blue corner like boxers in a ring

I was red and I lost this fight

my consciousness broke

great schizophrenic feeling of insecure

love triangle where whole town knew

bits of truth

I didn't care much for attention

you vapourised like a dream

striking my head from the inside

bizzarre that it still boiling in me

deep and strong

feeling that task is unresolved

until I will see again your smile

I lost everything forgot to keep the key

open operation transplantation of broken heart

still beating rythm of that song in the radio

after you go away

crazy times when I fell in schizophrenic love triangle

burned and destroyed bridges of my past

I keep your number like a treasure

to meet you again armoured with better attitude and

richer vocabulary sober life

a flow from my pure innocence when I fell with your eyes

since the first time

my burning mind show untouched yet

poisoned with acid rain crying over the city

screams of seagulls to pass the message

each step I've tried to made outside was milestone

of my stoned personal death

lost in time paradoxes when I met you on the street corner

so many times missed ocassions to start conversation

cos I feel like my head is empty basket for bunch of flowers

feeded in garden with special care to grow and glow

in the night as bright as my shining mind when think of you

I am mad in Stokes Croft

monk without shoes carries black milk to feed my students in a bottle

to send message through transmitters connecting our minds

somehow I can see you in rain drops

cool smoke

frustrating clouds visits
spinning head side behind leaf
skate beyond years as birds
source of contemplation
morning balancing memory
roots grow
burnt cornfields ripe life
sunshine layers reflect dusk
sealing ozon hole calls
dog walking away on hooked thorns
who shedding image longer
why did clusters moving slim
ready mistery body shapes
covers October refresh experience
journey jazz on warm tree
through paradise shade
sparkling green light loves
white dry reflection
watered jungle smoke cool
old hungry green nectar

dry milk

under creation of god we walk together as a couple

to find what was sin what was paradise. later when love is gone

left only dry milk on a dessert you can feed but your mouth will

fullfill terrible infant. again you are in a womb of this land

again you are in a womb of suicide. try to kill insect struggling

with your brain eating it to survive next day

serenity glow in the dark when full moon is on the sky

to big to care with bare eye

my clue stood up somewhere in a glaze who appeared

in front of me waking up of dreamers ball of psychiatric unit

they told me that we are a bunch of freaks ready to be shot by a system

which collapsed on our heads that new society is born

old structures keep an eye to save this world the same with victims of solitary

prophets to the new worlds of Devil rejected because she is too mad to lead

dig in a hole to find skeleton of my body on demand taken out of grave

to beat zombies attacking of every corner of this land

love eaten by seagulls petroleum floor under fire

cognitive resistance by leads on dog collars to prevent sentences

## four faced god

you said one day
you are somebody else
I loved all of you
Now I am standing without shoes
hope to find another cross
to use it as a crutch
my addictions my faith
in strenght of real love
my compassion for weakness
closed me again in a closet
I show up my face
as four faced forgotten God
all what is left is picture
taken that funny night
I felt like I own the city
the city is mine

glass mountains

all sudden illuminations of our souls ended
with suffocation for the purpose of money running
river of blood in banks of Avon George. I wander under
the bridge sitting in a cardboard box thinking about you
with homeless around the camp in wilderness
surrounding town don't mind distant ports never achieved
but my dog's sniffin nose finds everywhere smell of your lips
when touched me so soft twice to beat them in street fight.
Melody of cars passing by jumping suicidal wave of unhappy folks
I decided to set up fire in my room to destroy all signs of my
psychopathological concrete base for copycats instead
in the ecstasy of saxophone burning in the flame I play acid jazz
to carry snakes to the centre of the Earth to reach sun
in the black night sparkled amphetamine paths where my world
travel alone to find out if it is worth to be sentenced and locked in
madhouse. sexy nurse poison me with prescribed meds
to hold my burning mind
city of sick madmans landing in saucepans in Harbourside
to walk on a surface of water in the year of the monkey.
my sick mind tied as spaghetti pulled out all visions of godess
in your body incarnation. these walls hiding my screaming soul
to touch again glass of Mount Everest to die in hot lava of nepalese
earthquake where I am

to chose the right colour in a game like a Jigsaw another episode

prepared to be executed by mental police of clean society for my

suicidal trick of drinking turpentine

I pray for my sins on the top of the hill where I was settled with my horrors

insanity grave coffin long as my body and green grass of Victoria Park

shadows of ghosts coming out of basement

night neon life hiding heads of informal patients in a night shop collecting

spare coins to get booze in Bearpitt where all my friends sleep together

drunk on a naked ground

I am ink

my eye catch sharp edges of old photography

with nude body it drowns into light trapped in

become shadows when body brightening of silver

pearl shining mirroring light and dies into it

deep darkness -

there is no end of it

early morning

I can smell fresh ink of newspaper

printed with black letters like poem

black coffee as ink I drink smoke tobacco

creates blue grey circles around me

coffee darkenning awakes time frozen on photography

my eyes sucked into that perfect moment prints

of black and silver ink

I am ink

I am inky black universe

stars shine out like buttons of my paper suit

on the edge there is darkness of dead black universe

Tonight I am on a mission I am inside retrospection

oh sound and vision sliced into pieces as puzzles

by hand of God

I am God to squeeze out of it presence essence

nude body

injection projection

I’ve seen things heard voices exciting

pulling sting of needles out of veins out of butt ends

switching lights as eyes concrete jungles

feeded with sewers underneath skin of town

green flash of light hits in a head to synchronise

timewatch inside with Nature

city walls end with river eating ocean for lunch

fat drops of pollution covers ever Zion

dusty tramps lovers of travel outside system

perfectly working as clockwork watch

every clock have different time minutes to heartbeats

bited by hungry zombies rambling around

look into keyhole cosmic harmonies cling

metallic white paths

dummies wander all day to balance physics laws

with washed off thoughts

hoboes on the street queued to give blue blood in one blink of eye

oracle to say final word to turn back of chosen path

it’s impossible how constructions networks of eaten roots in mind

of establishment drains single views innocents to follow with sick ambitions for better life to forget simple joys

dividing hate with love

suicidal techniques to show sorrow and black hole in the head

forget grammar structures to keep on conversations breakdown inside

ears drilling alarm

woke me at noon

emergency state

drinking black coffee

isolate from inside

boil blood

contraband chewing gum

i miss a cigarette

its snowing outside

already spring

I am inside

on a side

in my bedsit I crave the world

lisergic acid

To dance with cloud

Imitate wind

Turning points on LSD vision

Orange bubble unlocks my head

Like astronauts glass helmet

Squatting festival of Woodstock

Lights concentrated in my eyes

Feet restless taps the rhythm

I was breathing moon inside chest

Hanging like a washing machine

On a string

Black milk drunk

Bushes population of creatures

Ants big like tractors

Living in my head

On a wall theater of shadows

Pissing boy kissing girls

I was lying on the grass

Blades cut my sight

Orange vision sweet taste

Bottle of crap wine ‘Byk’

Connection of buzzing body with Eternity

## love letter

how sick I am?

wanted by law

pure lies on my tongue

murals telling story to read from lips

I lost

hear music played by captured voices

how sick I am?

fingers spotted in hell

melted crystals of tears

glue my head to steel spot

painted with dark colour of wine

for our last supper

we had faces sprinkled with salt

white background for naked lunch

calls me every night I am trying to sleep

eye lids stays open like lids of coffin

quite dead me still calling you

lively colour to paint my dreams heavy with strong

language and sex scenes

fresh body bites for lunch

I wish

how sick I am without you here

I wish

came back bring remedy

I can’t find cure in someone else’s straitjacket

***

Holes in the fabric of Reality

where wind is whisking songs from radio

and talk to me

unseen

no money in my pocket

inside I am a rocket superwoman

to break the prison walls

my head wrapped with cotton

like Guantanamo kids

I am yours but no one knows

who is in me

I wear paper suit

no one recognise me on the street

## Blade Runner

creating rainbow bridge

that I know on the other side

is a real treasure to slide down

on a blade of rainbow made by prismatic

effect of broken glass which you throw

out when drunk

I was paralised to make right move to save

moment to remember scenes live theatre

we play main roles over the time

I stuck in that reality frozen into bunch of minutes

I could glue them together make a movie

and watch it again all over

to make it more clear or leave it like that

for my uncounscious mind

melody of my beating heart to the clear sky

when I am better with words to tell you

how I fell for you

in waterfall of emotional landscape

escape physically from my past

wishes of death surrounding my neck

with lines of words I can express more attention

for life new phrases coming to my head new order

encourage me to cut off the tree before I die

that time

I saw everything from different angle

wish this not scare anymore when town fall

of sleeping souls create epicentre of universe

city divided for two parts yours and mine

couldn't step outside my zone to tell you escalated

creepy thoughts that my imagination was killed with

bullets of ignorance

my brain torn for pieces as puzzles enlightened with smell

of your body. I am still in your kitchen watching you washing dishes

trying to make myself younger for you

inside I am still a child growing in a rain of

rainbow mushroom cloud

***

Imagine that

two women in a kitchen

one is cleaning kitchen table

spits to the glass

'This is how I am..' she says

She washes dishes other woman talks

'Would you shut up?' asks the first one

'I think you have to shut me up,' says the other one

Tension of electric phase makes both opposite poles
of the Earth untill they kiss
North Pole and South Pole melts in love breeze
each word a sun beam
labirynth of words built up from crystals and mirrors
to magnify in blinding sunlight mouth of God
whole truth of yourself disappearing behind the doors
the only way to clear all views at once
simple complex of ideal purity
black spot licked in tao sign
like old movie with silverskin girls
shining as pearls in shadows to have better view of the colour
white and light next to darkening shadows around persons
real love on a silverscreen drives you to madness
in a system of unreality

## she

your light cures dark skies

trembling hands of trees

lungs blowing smoky air

white storms of windy weather

under command of your eyes

pretty blue objects on pale horizon

possessions obsession

thoughts tied to one lost moment in time

heal me cure me

you’re the doctor for my sick soul

sangwinic temper cold heartaches

howling during phase of fool moon

to see you again

lunatic asylum ties me I insist to

break striped window

to get some air

speed of sound

I wonder how to undress colour to naked letter of poem

about pen and paper to touch invisible net of words to

subscribe untold yet construction of inner world build with

colours and letters

When I think of auras mixed in a crowd on crossroads when

red lights and people wait to hurry to the other side of the light

isn't it so obvious that human clock speeds to beat sound?

on a pavement stand still only beggars and collectors of hot air

steaming of city's sewers like skin sweats

jacked in matrix sunlight

system blocked with concrete armours suits of town centre

pinks and red oranges reflects surrounding sunrise each morning

not killed by traffic jam pollution poisons coming out of chimneys

factory melting human resource into meat

clockwork money energy

sign of contracts with devil capitalistic miracles from hell of
markets

this is your god

paper money

obey

boundries

buy

marry and have children

on a leash

of clean society

**Kinga Stefaniec**

I was born in 1980 in Radom, central Poland. I lived in small village where there was perfect background for a young child to grow up. Five years later I moved with my parents and younger brother to miner's town Zabrze in southern Poland where I started my education and I soaked atmosphere of mines, miners and silesian folks. My mother was a typist, so my childhood was filled with typing tapping in background. My first money I earned playing chess when I was eight years old. I graduated Silesian University in 2010. I studied Polish Literature paying more interest to theory of language and poetry. In 2008 emigrated from Poland to live in Bristol, England. Here I found my Kingdom. I do not know if this place will be my grave or I will move forward to another place, but I love that city and people living here. My profession is teaching and editing. In the past I done excellent job in probation in my home town in Poland where I worked with offenders helping them to straighten up their complicated lives. As English is not my mother tongue I find it satisfying to create world of my poetry with English language. My interest with poetry started in high school and till present day I polish my ability to put words into worlds. My master of poetry is Allen Ginsberg, but I find inspiration in other beatnik poets.

Queer, hitchhiker, bookworm and psychonaut. Always anxious when stay too long in one location, I prefer live nomad, gypsy life. My dream is to leave everything behind and start to travel all over the world in my camper van or hitchhike. I love to hitchhike on my own, I am not scared at all. It gives me feeling of freedom and adventure. I can afford to travel for free and see interesting places and meet amazing people on my way. So far I visited only Europe, but my dream is to go *furthur* to the edge of the world.

My other interests are photography, music, film, art, reading and collecting books, video games and stroking cats.

In 2016 and 2017 my art was exhibited in Southbank Centre in London, I was awarded platinum and bronze Koestler Awards twice for poetry. Another sample of my work is published online on Polish website www.gnosis.art.pl

Since 2015 I was admitted to mental hospital where I am till present day. In hospital I wrote most of my poetry who is telling the story of experiencing psychiatric ward. Simultanously I work now on my first novel.

Milton Keynes UK
Ingram Content Group UK Ltd.
UKHW041152231023
431175UK00001B/293